UNDERSTANDING THE
NONRELIGIOUS

BY CYNTHIA KENNEDY HENZEL

CONTENT CONSULTANT

Phil Zuckerman

Professor of Sociology and Secular Studies
Pitzer College

Essential Library

An Imprint of Abdo Publishing | abdopublishing.com

UNDERSTANDING WORLD RELIGIONS AND BELIEFS

ABDOPUBLISHING.COM

Published by Abdo Publishing, a division of ABDO, PO Box 398166, Minneapolis, Minnesota 55439. Copyright © 2019 by Abdo Consulting Group, Inc. International copyrights reserved in all countries. No part of this book may be reproduced in any form without written permission from the publisher. Essential Library™ is a trademark and logo of Abdo Publishing.

Printed in the United States of America, North Mankato, Minnesota
042018
092018

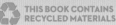
THIS BOOK CONTAINS RECYCLED MATERIALS

Cover Photo: Creative Travel Projects/Shutterstock Images
Interior Photos: Lisa Poole/AP Images, 4–5; Ginger Perry/The Winchester Star/AP Images, 6; Bettmann/Getty Images, 9, 34; Hrecheniuk Oleksii/Shutterstock Images, 14–15; Everett Art/Shutterstock Images, 18; Sergey Novikov/Shutterstock Images, 20–21; Georgios Kollidas/Shutterstock Images, 24; Time Life Pictures/LIFE Picture Collection/Getty Images, 26–27; Graham Corney/Shutterstock Images, 31; Fotosearch/Archive Photos/Getty Images, 37; Universal History Archive/Universal Images Group/Getty Images, 38–39; Levitin Mark/Shutterstock Images, 43; Shutterstock Images, 45, 47, 48–49, 52–53, 82–83; Edward Lara/Shutterstock Images, 55; Denise Lett/Shutterstock Images, 58–59; Eugenio Marongiu/Shutterstock Images, 60; Dragon Images/iStockphoto, 62–63; Monkey Business Images/iStockphoto, 65; David Cheskin/PA Images/Getty Images, 68–69; Tom Dodge/Columbus Dispatch/AP Images, 72–73; Anton Balazh/Shutterstock Images, 74–75; Juriaan Wossink/Shutterstock Images, 78; Akira Suemori/AP Images, 84–85; Brooks Kraft/Corbis Historical/Getty Images, 87; Charles Ommanney/Getty Images News/Getty Images, 88; Rex/Shutterstock, 92–93; Alastair Grant/AP Images, 96; Steven Senne/AP Images, 98–99

Editor: Arnold Ringstad
Series Designer: Maggie Villaume

LIBRARY OF CONGRESS CONTROL NUMBER: 2017961410

PUBLISHER'S CATALOGING-IN-PUBLICATION DATA

Name: Henzel, Cynthia Kennedy, author.
Title: Understanding the nonreligious / by Cynthia Kennedy Henzel.
Description: Minneapolis, Minnesota : Abdo Publishing, 2019. | Series: Understanding world religions and beliefs | Includes online resources and index.
Identifiers: ISBN 9781532114304 (lib.bdg.) | ISBN 9781532154133 (ebook)
Subjects: LCSH: Atheism--Juvenile literature. | Atheism--History--Juvenile literature. | World religions--Juvenile literature. | Religious belief--Juvenile literature.
Classification: DDC 211.8--dc23

CONTENTS

ESTABLISHMENT OF RELIGION

In 1956, 16-year-old Ellery Schempp walked into his high school in Abington, Pennsylvania, carrying a borrowed copy of the Koran. This is the holy book of Islam. It was the Monday after Thanksgiving. Ellery was a junior and an honor student looking forward to college, but today he was nervous. The action he was about to take would no doubt cause trouble. He had no idea what the consequences would be. But he knew he was doing the right thing.

The state of Pennsylvania required that ten verses from the King James Version of the Bible be read to the students each day. This was not uncommon at that time. Three dozen other states allowed reading from the Bible in public schools.[1] The states hoped that teaching moral lessons, such as the Ten Commandments of the Christian Bible, would help students become good citizens. Schools commonly began the day with prayers or hymns.

More than 60 years after his protest, Ellery Schempp is remembered for his involvement in a case about the separation of church and state.

The appropriateness of biblical readings and prayers in public schools continues to be a subject of debate today.

However, Ellery did not think this was right. He and his friends had discussed the First Amendment to the Constitution. Part of the amendment said that "Congress shall make no law respecting an establishment of religion."[2] This is known as the establishment clause. Public schools were supported by the government, so was it right that they promoted church activities?

Silent Protest

As the other students listened to Bible verses, Ellery quietly looked through the Koran. No one seemed to notice. A student came on the announcement system to lead the Lord's Prayer. As the other students stood to follow along, Ellery sat nervously in his seat. Everyone noticed that.

At the end of homeroom, the teacher asked Ellery if he was going to repeat his actions. When he said yes, she sent him to the principal. The principal accused him of being disrespectful of the school rules. He asked if Ellery was having problems at home. Ellery explained that he simply disagreed with Bible readings in school. The principal sent him to the school counselor to find out what was wrong with him.

The Establishment Clause

There was nothing wrong with Ellery. He simply believed that it was unconstitutional for the school to make students listen to passages from the Bible and pray each morning. The text of the First Amendment means that the government cannot support a religion or make laws favoring one belief system over another. Ellery felt it was obvious that forcing students to listen to readings from a Christian Bible and say Christian prayers in a public school showed that the government had a preference for one religion. He thought that if he pointed out this problem, the adults would take care of it.

STANDING FOR CIVIL RIGHTS

The American Civil Liberties Union (ACLU) was founded in 1919 in response to the US government's roundup of people believed to have Communist sympathies. People were arrested and deported with no regard for their rights of due process of law or restrictions on search and seizure, both part of the Bill of Rights. A small group of people decided to stand up for the constitutional rights of the accused. Since that time, the ACLU has been a defender of the civil rights of people across the United States, even when the views of the people it defends are viewed by the public as wrong or hateful.

Ellery belonged to the Unitarian Universalists, a church that was open to all types of ideas. Some of his friends were of the Jewish faith. Others belonged to different faiths or were nonreligious. The Bible readings made them all uncomfortable, but his friends were afraid to protest against the school. Some felt it might make it harder to get into a university. Others feared what their parents would say if they stood up against the school officials.

Ellery's parents supported him. They suggested he write to the American Civil Liberties Union (ACLU), an organization that supports people who feel their civil liberties are being violated. Ellery wrote the letter. He had no idea at the time that his protest would take him and his family to the US Supreme Court.

Ellery, *second from right*, posed for a photo with his family in front of the Supreme Court after his case finally reached the court in 1963.

A Long Fight

Those years were not easy for Ellery's family. As the family waited for the case, *School District of Abington Township v. Schempp*, to move through the courts, Ellery graduated from high school. Since he was no longer in school, he could not protest school rules that did not affect him. His parents, along with his younger brother and sister who were still in school, became plaintiffs in the case. The family received hate mail. Someone smeared excrement on their door. His brother was bullied and his sister was teased. Other kids called their home the "Commie camp," meaning the family must be in league with the atheist, Communist enemies of the United States. The principal of the high school wrote letters to the universities where Ellery applied. He recommended that the universities not admit Ellery because he was a troublemaker.

In 1963, the Supreme Court made its ruling in *School District of Abington Township v. Schempp*. Justice Tom C. Clark, writing for the 8–1 majority opinion, found that the "opening exercise is a religious ceremony, and was intended by the State to be so."[3] Because of that, the court ruled that the Bible-verse exercises and the law requiring them were in violation of the establishment clause. The Schempp family had won.

Outrage

In the United States, many people feel their religion is intertwined with culture and day-to-day life. Many people were outraged by the court's decision. Some believed that the United States was founded on Christian values and that those values should remain at the forefront in the nation's laws. They believed that taking the Bible and prayer out of the classroom was abandoning God and faith, as well as the history and culture of the country. The outrage had been similar the year before, when the Supreme Court had ruled in *Engel v. Vitale* that nondenominational prayers written by government officials for use in school were promoting religion.

With the *Engel v. Vitale* case settling the issue of prayer in school and Ellery's own case settling the issue of Bible readings, Ellery hoped that the issue of religion in schools was finished. During the next years, he earned degrees in physics and geology from Tufts University. He then earned a PhD in physics from Brown University and went on to have a significant career in science.

SCHEMPP THE SCIENTIST

Schempp went on to earn a doctoral degree and had a long career as a physicist. One of his jobs was with the General Electric Corporation. He worked for eight years developing a new technology, the magnetic resonance imaging (MRI) system, for use in medical diagnosis. It is extremely useful for looking inside the body. Today, this tool is being used to study the human brain and how it processes beliefs.

ENGEL V. VITALE

Steven Engel was shocked when he looked into his son's elementary school classroom. His hands clasped and his head bent, his son was following the teacher, who was leading the prayer: "Almighty God, we acknowledge our dependence upon Thee, and we beg Thy blessings upon us, our parents, our teachers and our Country."[4] This was not the way the Jewish father had taught his son to pray.

Engel, along with four other parents, including both religious and nonreligious people, sued the school board for requiring students to recite the nondenominational prayer that had been written by the school board. In 1962, the Supreme Court ruled in *Engel v. Vitale* that the First Amendment to the US Constitution prohibited public schools from requiring school prayer due to the school's government funding.

Not the End

The fight to keep religion and schools separate was not over. The Supreme Court heard many more cases dealing with religion in schools and public spaces. Some of them addressed praying in school or at school-sponsored events. The court found that holding public prayers before high school football games was unconstitutional in a 1995 decision, *Santa Fe Independent School District v. Doe*.

Other Supreme Court cases considered what can be taught in school. Religious parents sometimes do not want children exposed to scientific theories, such as evolution, when those theories contradict religious teachings. In 1968, the court ruled in *Epperson v. Arkansas* that schools could not ban the teaching of evolution. Schools then attempted to teach the concept of intelligent design, the belief that such an orderly universe must have had a creator or designer. The Supreme Court ruled in

2005 in *Kitzmiller et al. v. Dover Area School District* that schools could not order the teaching of intelligent design.

For the nonreligious, as well as those in minority religions, the Supreme Court rulings prevented schools from indoctrinating their children into beliefs the parents did not agree with. The Supreme Court had maintained that "no religion" is a belief system protected under the Constitution just like belief systems of faith.

The nonreligious are a diverse group, and they have a broad range of beliefs and philosophies. Some do not believe in a god. Others are uncertain about whether a god exists. And some believe in a higher power but do not identify with any established religions. The first challenge with understanding the nonreligious is to identify these important distinctions.

RELIGIOUS SYMBOLS ON PUBLIC LAND

Outside of schools, a battle has been waged over whether the government-sanctioned display of religious items violates the First Amendment. Court battles have been waged over Christmas displays on public property, statues of the Ten Commandments on courthouse lawns, and crosses erected in national parks. The Supreme Court has not provided any clear guidance on this issue. In some cases, the court has approved scenes depicting the birth of Jesus that were surrounded by more secular holiday items, while in other cases the court has forced communities to remove such scenes when they were seen as promoting religion. The Supreme Court, nearly equally divided between conservatives and liberals, has had to decide case by case which public displays are primarily historical or secular and which are promoting religion.

Nonreligious people come from all cultures and all walks of life.

CHAPTER TWO

WHO ARE THE NONRELIGIOUS?

When people filled out a US Census survey in 2008, they were asked to identify their religions. They could select among well-known religions such as Catholicism, Protestantism, Islam, Hinduism, or Buddhism, as well as less well-known religions. Those who didn't belong to an established religion could select among the nonreligious categories of "atheist," "agnostic," "humanist," or "no religion."[1] With all these labels and options, what does it mean to be nonreligious?

Those who are nonreligious are not all the same. Some of them go to churches, temples, or mosques. They may even be members of an established religion while not believing in the strict doctrine of the faith. Many of them celebrate religious holidays as part of their cultures or family traditions. Some of them may not participate in any established religion but still believe in some spiritual beings. Others are outspoken about their lack of belief in anything supernatural.

Historically, many people who are nonreligious have not been open about their lack of religious belief because being nonreligious has long been viewed negatively by the religious majority. The nonreligious may be seen as ungodly, amoral people who may face punishment after death. In many places, this is still true today. In the United States, polling has shown that atheists are one of the least trusted minorities among the general public. The majority of Americans also use religious belief as an indicator of how moral a person is. A 2011 survey indicated that more than one-half of Americans think morality requires a belief in God.[2]

Early Views on the Nonreligious

Intolerance toward those who question established religions has existed since ancient times. Early Sophists, or traveling teachers of ancient Greece, encouraged their students to question common beliefs. Protagoras (490–420 BCE) wrote about how he could find no definitive answers about the

STOICISM

Many philosophies that flourished in ancient Greece and Rome were based on personal growth. The philosophy of Stoicism, founded by Zeno of Citium, taught self-control and internal strength as means of overcoming destructive emotions. Today the word *stoic* refers to someone who has the quality of enduring pain or hardship without complaint.

nature of the gods: "Concerning the gods I am not in a position to know either that (or how) they are or that (or how) they are not, or what they are like in appearance."[3]

The Greek philosopher Socrates (470–399 BCE) believed that reason, rather than religion, should be used to establish ethics and laws. He talked about his philosophy on the streets of Athens. He did not preach. Instead, he developed a system of asking questions to get people to reflect on their beliefs rather than simply accepting what they were told by authorities. This became known as the Socratic method.

The authorities in Athens did not like Socrates challenging their power or questioning the gods. Socrates was charged with corrupting the youth of the city. He was put on trial, found guilty, and sentenced to death. The first recorded use of the term *atheist*, meaning one who was not a theist, or believer in gods, was by Socrates, in an account of his trial written by his student Plato (427–347 BCE).

THE DEATH OF SOCRATES

Socrates, having been found guilty by the authorities in Athens, was sentenced to death. Following tradition, he was asked if he would recommend another punishment. He might have avoided the death penalty if he had suggested exile from the city, but instead he sarcastically suggested he should be rewarded. When pressed, he suggested he pay a small fine. He did not want to be banned from the city he loved, and he did not fear death. The jury decided on the original sentence. Socrates died from drinking hemlock, a powerful poison.

A famous painting by the French artist Jacques Louis David (1748–1825) depicts the moments before Socrates drinks the poison that carries out his death sentence.

A new religion, Christianity, arose after the death of its central figure, Jesus, in the first century CE. Another major faith, Islam, was established by Muhammad in the 600s CE. These two religions became dominant in Europe and the Middle East. Unlike the earlier Greek religion, they were monotheistic. This meant followers worshipped a single god, rather than a large number of gods.

The Middle Ages, from approximately 500 to 1400, are sometimes called the Age of Faith. The Roman Catholic Church, a major branch of Christianity, gained enormous power. Most people during the Middle Ages were uneducated. They could not read the Bible themselves and did not question church teachings. Nonbelievers were heavily persecuted by the church.

Free Thought Emerges

People who questioned the prevailing religions have been found throughout history. The Charvaka of India were people who defied the Vedas, the oldest scripture of Hinduism. They believed that the mind was not separate from the body, so when the body dies the mind ceases to exist.

Wang Chong (25–100 CE) questioned the prevalent superstitions and understanding of science in ancient China. He wrote essays about physics, astronomy, and philosophy. Although not widely read during his lifetime, his work was revived in the 1800s and 1900s both in China and in the West.

The Middle East also contributed early religious skeptics. Born in Baghdad, Ibn ar-Rawandi (died 910 CE) was an atheist who used reason to argue against many of the tenets of Islam. He claimed that

Florence's famous cathedral, which dates back to the Renaissance era, still stands today.

the Koran was not the word of God and that prophets were similar to magicians, resulting in his condemnation by clerics.

Al-Razi (died 925 CE) was a Persian physician born in what is now the country of Iran. He was the most famous physician of the Middle Ages. Al-Razi denied many of the tenets of the dominant Muslim faith, such as the existence of prophets who were set above other people by God, and he was called a heretic. Many of his philosophical writings were destroyed, but those that remained, along with his valuable medical work, would become influential in Europe.

End of the Middle Ages

In Europe, attitudes toward the nonreligious began to change during the Renaissance. This period, lasting from the 1300s to the 1600s, was marked by major advances in art, science, and philosophy. Slowly, the growth of free thought began. The first of these moves toward religious freedom began in Italy.

The city of Florence, Italy, was one of the wealthiest places in the world at the beginning of the 1300s. Wealthy people became patrons of artists. They collected art and manuscripts from the ancient Greeks and Romans. As these ancient texts and philosophies were rediscovered, thinkers began to view the world in a new way.

This new way of thinking gave rise to humanism. Humanism is a viewpoint that centers on people instead of God. Humanists viewed all religions as having common values. They emphasized the idea that people's lives do not revolve around sin and redemption, but that humans have dignity. They believed that people could control nature. Humanists developed a new body of knowledge apart from that presented in religious texts. They believed that science and reason could create an ethical society without morals being handed down from a higher or heavenly authority. From Italy, the Renaissance and the idea of humanism spread throughout Europe.

Asking Questions

The Renaissance was a new age of thought. Humanism encouraged curiosity and questioning of the world. Leonardo da Vinci (1452–1519), the famous painter and sculptor, studied the science of flight and human anatomy. Sir Francis Bacon (1561–1626) devised a methodology of experimenting to draw conclusions. This would later become the scientific method. Galileo (1564–1642) experimented to determine the physical laws that dictate how objects move. He explored space with a telescope.

New discoveries and ideas flourished. But the Catholic Church continued to hold enormous power in Europe. There was often little difference between religion and government. Governments typically had established religions. Church leaders were powerful forces in government. Some kings, including Louis XIV of France (1638–1715), believed in the divine right of kings. This was the concept that a monarch derived the right to rule directly from God. A monarch did not have to answer to any other authority.

Heavenly Troubles

Galileo's investigations soon got him into trouble when he defended a theory of Copernicus (1473–1543), an earlier mathematician and astronomer. Copernicus had proposed that Earth circled the sun, contradicting the prevailing belief that the sun rotated around Earth. Church doctrine held that God created man and Earth as the center of the universe. Following the Bible rather than scientific studies, the church authorities came down on the side of an Earth-centric universe.

Since Galileo's theory went against church doctrine, he was arrested for heresy and threatened with torture and death if he did not reverse his statements. Although he said, "I do not believe

LEONARDO DA VINCI

Leonardo da Vinci was perhaps one of the most intelligent people who ever lived. He was an artist, architect, scientist, and philosopher. He created some of the world's most famous religious paintings, including *The Last Supper*. Yet his scientific curiosity caused him to question stories from the Bible, such as the great flood of the Old Testament. Whether Leonardo was Christian, agnostic, or atheist remains unknown.

Galileo, punished in his time for heresy, would later be seen as a symbol of resistance to religious dogma.

GALILEO PARDONED

The Catholic Church's stance on the fixed position of Earth was taken from the story of creation in the Bible: "God fixed the Earth upon its foundation, not to be moved forever." After the ruling against Galileo, the scientist is said to have muttered, "Even so, it does move," though it's possible this phrase was an invention of later writers.[5] When Galileo died in 1642, he was still under house arrest. Centuries later, in 1984, a committee for the Roman Catholic Church presented its findings on the case of Galileo. After 13 years of study, the church admitted that Galileo had been correct in his theory and had been falsely condemned. Pope John Paul II formally admitted the mistake in 1992.

that the same God who has endowed us with senses, reason and intellect has intended us to forgo their use," he finally confessed to heresy to avoid being burned at the stake.[4] The church convicted him and sentenced him to house arrest. Taking any stance that was counter to religious belief was an unpopular or even dangerous choice during this time. But in the coming centuries, views on nonreligious belief would continue to shift.

BREAKING THE LINK BETWEEN CHURCH AND STATE

In the midst of the Renaissance era, the Catholic Church was accused of corruption. Under the Catholic doctrine, priests could help the faithful find forgiveness from God for their sins. However, by the 1500s, the church had begun the practice of forgiving sins for a price. Money could buy an indulgence, or forgiveness of a sin.

Martin Luther, a German Catholic monk, was shocked by this and other concerns he had about the church establishment. He believed that by pointing out the problems, he could get the church to fix

Martin Luther's questioning of mainstream religion opened the door for widespread doubts about religious doctrines.

itself. In 1517, he published his protests in a document known as the Ninety-Five Theses. In response, the church banished Luther as a heretic.

Luther then translated the Bible into German and continued publishing pamphlets containing his ideas. Johannes Gutenberg's invention of the printing press in the mid-1400s allowed Luther to share his ideas widely. Luther's free thought eventually created a break within the Catholic Church. This was the beginning of the Protestant Reformation (1517–1648), a movement that encouraged people to read and interpret the Bible for themselves. Separate sects of Christianity began breaking away from the Catholic Church.

Martin Luther and the Lutherans, his followers, were not atheists or even nonreligious. They were Christians who felt that the leaders of the Catholic Church had lost their way. But they established the idea that people could think for themselves when interpreting the Bible. They did not have to blindly follow the teachings of the largest church.

The Catholic Church soon cracked down on dissenters. In a process called the Roman Inquisition, it violently persecuted those with ideas that went against church doctrine. People against the Roman Catholic Church, or Protestants, arose in northern Europe and England. The Thirty Years' War (1618–1648), waged between Catholic and Protestant forces, tore Germany apart.

The Enlightenment

As the destructive Thirty Years' War ended, scientists and philosophers once again began studying the world. Scientists began to search for natural explanations for how the world worked. Based on work from the Renaissance, scientists refined the scientific method. Isaac Newton (1643–1727) used this work to describe the physics of motion and light and to lay the groundwork for a scientific revolution.

The philosopher John Locke (1632–1704) used the principles of reason to argue that truth could be found through human thinking and logic rather than an outside authority. He developed a political theory of government by the consent of the governed. He proposed the notion of religious tolerance, the basis for the separation of church and state. This period of scientific and philosophical innovation became known as the Enlightenment.

THE ROMAN INQUISITION

The Roman Inquisition was used by the Roman Catholic Church to control heretics. Earlier inquisitions, which began in the Middle Ages, were known for finding and violently suppressing heresy in the general population. The Roman Inquisition, contending with the spread of Protestant ideas, focused on heresy committed by more educated people. One outcome of the Roman Inquisition was the compilation of the first Index of Forbidden Books—a list of books banned by the church—in 1559.

RATIONALISM AND HUMANISM

Rationalism and humanism are related concepts, though they have separate, specific meanings. Rationalism has its roots in science. The primary goal of a rationalist is to use reason and logic to answer questions. Rationalists require evidence to come to logical conclusions. Rationalists believe that all human beings have fundamental rights. They believe in a society in which individuals are free to practice their own beliefs.

Humanists believe that human experience and rational thought provide a moral code to live by. Religious beliefs are not necessary for people to live ethical lives, and a moral code comes from lessons of history, personal experience, and thought. As do rationalists, humanists believe there are no supernatural beings. The material universe is the only thing that exists, and science provides the only reliable source of knowledge about the universe.

Another Enlightenment philosopher, David Hume (1711–1776), used Locke's work combined with the scientific method of Isaac Newton to investigate how the mind works in acquiring knowledge. Hume became known for his skepticism, questioning the reality of anything that could not be directly experienced.

The Age of Reason

Thomas Paine's 1794 book *The Age of Reason* is said to be the most influential text in atheism, although Paine himself was not an atheist. He argued for deism, the belief that established religions and the Bible did not prove the existence of God. Deists rejected the Bible and other religious texts as the revealed word of God. They did not believe the idea that God worked miracles or interfered in human events.

Paine is remembered today for his contributions to humanism and his role in helping inspire the American Revolution.

However, deists did not argue against the existence of God. They believed God created the universe. They also believed God gave men the ability to reason. Paine argued that only reason and observation of the natural world could prove the existence of a divine creator. Paine had published his ideas in pamphlets prior to the publication of his book. In 1776, Thomas Jefferson penned the Declaration of Independence using many of Paine's ideas.

A Christian Nation

Freedom of religion was not the norm in the early history of America. Many European colonists had come to North America seeking freedom to worship as they wanted. But that did not mean that they believed in freedom of religion for everyone in their colony. A group called the Puritans established their own strict religion in the Massachusetts Bay Colony. People of other religions faced the death penalty there.

THOMAS JEFFERSON

There has long been controversy over the religious beliefs of Thomas Jefferson. He was raised in the Anglican Church and believed in a supreme being, but he questioned religious dogma. He was an Enlightenment scholar who wrote to his nephew, "Question with boldness even the existence of a god; because, if there be one, he must more approve the homage of reason, than that of blindfolded fear."[2]

Other colonies gave preference to Catholics or members of other religions. Religion and family were closely linked. In 1683, the colony of Pennsylvania required parents to teach their children to read and write "so they may be able to read the Scriptures."[1] By 1775, the year before the writing of the Declaration of Independence, nine of the colonies had some type of established church.

Thomas Jefferson realized that the colonies could not be united if religious differences set them against each other. He and others proposed a separation of church and state, allowing everyone to worship as they chose with no interference from the government. Taxes would not support one religion over another. This separation was the basis for the establishment clause of the US Constitution.

Darwin's Explanation

Science continued to progress in the 1800s, and with these advances came more skepticism of religion. Charles Darwin (1809–1882) was born into a wealthy English family with a background in science. His father was a medical doctor and his grandfather was a botanist. Darwin had an early interest in exploring nature. After completing college, he signed on as a naturalist on the British ship *Beagle* in 1831 for a five-year journey to explore the world. During the voyage he collected many plant and animal specimens. He began to notice similarities and differences between specimens from different locations.

As Darwin wrote up his findings after the trip, he developed a new theory about how various species developed on Earth. The result of his research was the theory of evolution. The theory proposed that species changed over time based on the conditions in which they lived. The process through which this happened was called natural selection. Animals with traits that were advantageous to their survival thrived, while others did not. Because those animals survived, their traits were naturally selected by the process of evolution. They were able to pass their traits on to the next

Darwin's study of tortoises, finches, and other species helped him develop his theory of evolution.

generation. Over many generations, this process can lead to significant changes. Because humans are animals, too, the theory of evolution also applied to them.

Darwin published his theory in his book *On the Origin of Species* in 1859. The theory was sensational. For scientists, it explained previous observations that had gone unexplained. It opened a whole new field of investigation.

But for many religious people, the theory was inflammatory. It directly contradicted the biblical doctrine that God created all things just as they are today. Though the scientific evidence for evolution is now overwhelming, many people today continue to object to it for religious reasons.

THE SCOPES MONKEY TRIAL

In 1925, high school teacher John Scopes was accused of breaking the laws of Tennessee. He was teaching evolution in his classroom rather than creationism. His trial became a great spectacle as two famous attorneys, Clarence Darrow for the defense and William Jennings Bryan for the prosecution, faced off in court. The case became known as the Scopes Monkey Trial. Early in the trial, the judge ruled that expert scientific testimony was not allowed. Darrow tried a new tactic. He brought Bryan to the stand. He ridiculed Bryan's fundamentalist interpretation of the Bible with his questions. Bryan, a three-time candidate for president of the United States, was humiliated. Still, Scopes was found guilty, but the case was overturned on a technicality. It wasn't until 1968 that the Supreme Court decided a similar case, *Epperson v. Arkansas,* in favor of teaching evolution.

NONRELIGIOUS WOMEN

Women in the early fight for women's rights included many nonreligious individuals. Ernestine Rose (1810–1892) was born in Poland into a Jewish family. Her father, a rabbi, arranged her marriage to a Jewish man when she was 16. She professed that she did not believe in Judaism and did not want to marry the man her father chose. When she was not allowed to break the engagement, she took the case to court, won, and went to England, where she helped create an atheist organization in 1835. Rose moved to the United States the next year and became a popular speaker fighting for women's rights and the abolition of slavery. Rose insisted that women's rights were human rights.

Elmina D. Slenker (1827–1909) was an outspoken atheist who wrote novels and short stories for children. Slenker also offered advice to women on the subjects of sex and marriage. She was arrested in 1887 for mailing letters advising women on how to avoid pregnancy.

Ernestine Rose was an early nonreligious advocate for women's rights.

Elizabeth Cady Stanton (1815–1902) also fought for equal rights for women. She helped organize the Seneca Falls Convention of 1848, the first women's rights convention. Stanton, who was anti-religious, broke with other suffragettes on issues of liberal divorce laws and a woman's right to reproductive determination. Her book *The Women's Bible* detailed how religion suppressed the rights of women.

Biologist Thomas Huxley invented the term *agnostic*, which is still in widespread use today.

CHAPTER FOUR

AGNOSTICS AND ATHEISTS

Darwin, like most scientists of his time, had grown up in a religious household. His family was Anglican, and Darwin had once considered becoming a clergyman. He knew that his new theory would not be well received in the religious community.

Many scientists at that time did not see science and religion as enemies. Rather, they thought that the methods of science could be applied to gain a greater understanding of the natural world as created by a higher power. Thomas Edison (1847–1931), one of the most famous inventors of the late 1800s, was not an atheist. Like many of the time, he criticized established religions but still believed in a higher intelligence. He said in a letter, "What you call God I call Nature, the Supreme intelligence that rules matter."[1]

As the debate raged on, more people began to believe that science might not be able to fully explain the universe. There was

A NEW WORD

After much thought and study about what he believed or did not believe about religion, Thomas Huxley decided that while others may think they had solved the problem of existence, he did not believe the issue was solvable. As he explained, "So I took thought, and invented what I conceived to be the appropriate title of 'agnostic.'" The word was the opposite of *gnostic*, an ancient Greek word meaning "to have knowledge." "To my great satisfaction," said Huxley, "the term took."[3]

no scientific evidence that God existed, as theists believed. Yet no one had scientifically proven that gods didn't exist, as atheists believed. Thomas Huxley, a biologist and one of Darwin's greatest defenders, believed that the lack of evidence on either side meant that a new term was needed: *agnostic*. An agnostic person thinks that the fact of whether there is a god or not is simply unknowable. Agnosticism addresses knowledge rather than belief. Although raised as an Anglican, Darwin began to doubt parts of his religion as he got older. He wrote, "The mystery of the beginning of all things is insoluble by us; and I for one must be content to remain an Agnostic."[2]

Others in Britain were committed to free thought. Charles Bradlaugh (1833–1891) was editor of the *National Reformer*, which was prosecuted for blasphemy. Along with George Holyoake, who coined the term *secular*, he founded the National Secular Society in 1866. Bradlaugh was elected to the House of Commons in 1880 but was denied taking his seat for five years because he refused to take the oath on a Bible. Holyoake was the last person in England who was imprisoned for atheism.

The Rise of Atheism

As the religious debate continued into the 1900s, another battle began in the political realm. Karl Marx (1818–1883), the German philosopher who helped develop the economic theories behind Communism, wrote that "religion is the opium of the people."[4] This was interpreted to mean that religion was used to subjugate the poor by giving them false hopes for something better in the afterlife.

PANTHEISM

The term *pantheism* was first used by Irish philosopher John Toland in 1705, but the idea of pantheism comes from ancient times. Pantheism is the belief that all of reality, including the forces and laws of the universe, is the equivalent of a god. This viewpoint denies the existence of a god who has an identity separate from the universe. Pantheists today emphasize respect for the rights of all living things and focus on protecting the natural world.

The 1900s brought the establishment of Communist governments in the Soviet Union and China. Although neither of these new Communist governments banned religion outright, Communist Party members were expected to profess atheism. Religion was discouraged.

Atheism under Communism

Atheism in the Soviet Union and China was not a choice of the individual. Rather than resulting from an individual's free thought, atheism was imposed on people by the government. The establishment of atheism in the Soviet Union protected the government from the power of the Russian Orthodox Church. In China, the new doctrine replaced the following of Confucius, an early Chinese philosopher who espoused a humanistic philosophy of morality.

Under Joseph Stalin in the Soviet Union and Mao Zedong in China, religions were brutally persecuted. During the 1920s and 1930s, religious leaders in the Soviet Union were shot or sent to work camps. By 1939, only approximately 500 of the 50,000 churches in the country were still open.[5]

RUSSIA AND CHINA TODAY

The Soviet Union dissolved into several separate countries in 1991. The largest of these is Russia. Polls have found that the number of atheists in Russia is declining. A poll conducted by the Russian independent research center Levada found that the portion of Russians who identified as atheists fell from 26 percent in 2014 to 13 percent in 2017.[6] On the other hand, other countries that had been under Soviet influence, such as the Czech Republic, have become some of the most atheist countries in the world. In 2008, 40 percent of Czechs were atheist and 15 percent were agnostic.[7] China is still heavily atheist, with approximately half of its people identifying as such.[8]

To this day, huge posters of Mao Zedong look down upon public places in China.

During a period known as the Cultural Revolution (1966–1976), Mao tried to purge traditional beliefs by persecuting millions of people across China who did not fall into line behind his new philosophy.

Though these nations lacked traditional gods, their founders or leaders took on the status of religious icons. They created personality cults around their own images. Through use of propaganda, Stalin took on the godlike characteristics of perfection and infallibility. Statues of him stood in public spaces around the nation. In China, Mao became almost a godlike figure for many people. His portraits looked down upon people across China.

THE CULT OF KIM

North Korea is one of few remaining Communist nations. Like some other nations founded under Communism, North Korea is run by a dictator who has established a godlike public image and personality cult despite an official policy of atheism. Kim Il-Sung took power in 1948. He was succeeded by his son Kim Jong-Il in 1994, who was in turn succeeded by his own son Kim Jong-Un in 2011. Each member of the Kim family has been honored and worshipped as a god.

God and the Cold War

In the 1950s, as these large Communist countries gained power, they came into conflict with Western democracies. This was especially true of the rivalry between the Soviet Union and the United States, the two most powerful countries at that time. The Cold War emerged between the two nations. This was a time of increasing tension and nuclear armament by both countries.

One of the ways that the United States differentiated itself from the Soviet Union was

Since the 1950s, the phrase "In God We Trust" has appeared on American bills.

in religion. The Soviet Union was seen as a godless state, whereas many in the United States viewed themselves as part of a Christian nation. Being Christian was equated with being a patriotic American. In 1954, the United States added the phrase "under God" to the Pledge of Allegiance to underline this difference.[9] The phrase "In God We Trust" was adopted as the national motto in 1956, and it was added to the country's currency.[10]

Keeping Quiet

Because of such negative feelings toward the nonreligious in the United States, atheists and agnostics have long been reluctant to reveal their thoughts to family, friends, or coworkers. In especially religious or conservative communities, such people run the risk of being shunned. Their families may even reject them or stop talking to them.

Many nonreligious people continue to enjoy the cultural aspects of religious holidays such as Christmas and Easter. Participating in gift exchanges and Easter egg hunts is common. Many of these people see no harm in people having religious faith even if they do not personally agree with those beliefs. Research shows that although the religious prefer the company of other religious people, the nonreligious show no preference as to whether someone is religious or nonreligious. Some nonreligious people even feel that religion, like popular fables, can be a good way to teach young children about morals. For most of history, nonreligious people have often kept their beliefs largely to themselves due to pressures from family and community or even for their own safety.

Some traditions, such as Easter egg hunts, have become unlinked from their religious roots.

THE NONRELIGIOUS REVIVAL

Today's nonreligious adhere to a variety of philosophies and outlooks. They may identify as rationalists, or those who believe that logic and science supersede faith. They may be humanists, or those who believe that people can live ethical lives without the commandments of a higher being. Others may be ardent atheists who believe that religious faith is a root cause of many of the world's problems. Many do not heed any defined belief system.

No matter the specific label, "no religion" is the fastest-growing religion-related category in the United States and many other countries. In the 1990 US Census, 14,331,000 people identified as having "no religion." By the time of a 2008 survey, that number had grown to 34,169,000—a 138 percent growth in only 18 years.[1]

Some nonreligious people find beauty in nature rather than in religious teachings.

The nonreligious are now the second-largest category of people in the United States and in much of Europe. Today, they make up approximately one-fourth of the total population in the United States.[2] Some European countries have even greater numbers. A 2014 survey in England and Wales found that 48.5 percent identified themselves as "nones."[3]

The nonreligious may be any age, gender, race, or nationality. Some come from religious families and left a religion after being raised in it. Others were raised in secular families. Some decide to leave a religion as a conscious choice, while others may simply drift away from a church, mosque, or other religious community over time.

Even the beliefs of those who identify as nonreligious are very different. Some may simply not think or care about religion at all. Others may be dedicated atheists, arguing against religious beliefs. Still others may believe in a god or other spiritual being but not identify with any organized religion. These people may consider themselves to be spiritual but not religious. All these variations mean that the population of nonreligious people is extremely diverse.

Why People Leave Religions

What religion people are raised with generally determines the religion they practice. Jews teach their children the tenets and rituals of their faith. So do Catholics, Muslims, and members of other religions. Teaching children about their religion or personal beliefs is one way parents instill morals. Religion is often tied closely to family activities, such as going to a house of worship, attending a religious camp,

NONRELIGIOUS AFRICAN AMERICANS

African Americans in the United States are more likely to be religious than whites. According to Pew research from 2008, 88 percent of African Americans definitely believed in God compared with 71 percent of the overall population.[7] More than one-half of African Americans attended church every week. Black churches have historically played a prominent role in the fight for civil rights. Many civil rights leaders, including the Reverend Martin Luther King Jr., were members of the clergy.

Because of these close religious ties, it is particularly difficult for some members of the black community to come out as nonreligious. Ronnelle Adams, author of the children's book *Aching and Praying*, wrote about the difficulty of telling his beloved and very religious grandmother that he was an atheist. He had already told his mother—and that had not gone well. They were not speaking at all. Although his grandmother took the news without condemnation, Adams knew she was disappointed in him. Still, they managed to maintain a relationship. For Adams, that was a win. As he said, "Where there was once vagary and silence on my beliefs . . . there's now clarity and silence. I still have my grandmother despite the tradition that I'm contending with."[8]

and having holiday events and family get-togethers. Historically, most people were raised in religious households. Of those born between 1925 and 1943, before the cultural changes brought by World War II (1939–1945), only 4 percent were raised with no religion.[4]

The number of people raised with no religion is now increasing. Of those born between 1971 and 1992, 11 percent were raised in nonreligious homes.[5] Just as people raised in a religion tend to adopt that religion, people who are raised in nonreligious households tend to be nonreligious. Less than 5 percent of adults with nonreligious parents join a religion.[6]

If children are raised in a religion, they often continue following that religion into adulthood.

Still, the majority of people who are nonreligious were raised in religious homes. People who leave an established religion are known as apostates. Because religion has historically been so intertwined with culture, and still is in many places, becoming an apostate was often the equivalent of being kicked out of a culture. For centuries, it was against the law to be nonreligious in many Western societies, and atheists continue to face discrimination. Still, many people today are choosing to leave a religion for intellectual, emotional, or social reasons.

Free Thought

Just as free thought led many people in the past to question the tenets of their religion, the choice to become nonreligious for many people is an intellectual decision. As children become teenagers and then young adults, they may begin to question the religion they were raised with. Most nonreligious adults left their religion between the ages of 16 and 25, a time when parents begin having less authority over their children's actions and beliefs. People often begin to read and travel more widely. They are exposed to different ideas and cultures. They make friends or even marry outside their faith.

As young people learn more about science, they find that the stories and beliefs they were raised with have no hard evidence to support them. Scientific evidence often contradicts the tenets of religious beliefs. These people may come to see religions as based on myth, not reality. They may give more credence to what is based on evidence than what is based on faith. These people may find that their ideas gradually change. They may leave behind their religions just as they left behind beliefs in things such as Santa Claus or the tooth fairy.

SKEPTICISM

Skeptics are those who question ideas, especially ones that are commonly held. Skeptics seek evidence to justify beliefs and ideas, rather than relying on instructions from authorities. They work to develop logical, rational reasoning for the things they believe. Skeptics often apply these methods to claims of the paranormal or supernatural. This may include mainstream beliefs, such as the existence of God, or more fringe beliefs, such as a belief in ghosts or psychics.

A Personal God

Some nonreligious people make the choice to leave a religion after a traumatic event in their lives. A death in the family, a serious illness, or another tragedy may cause people to lose their faith in a personal God that watches over them. They may question whether prayers are heard or how a

For some, studying a religious text strengthens their faith. For others, this kind of close reading drives a person away from religion.

PERSPECTIVES

LEARNING TO THINK

Cora Judd was raised in a strict Mormon household. As a child and later as a young woman, she felt pressure to become a more perfect Mormon. She prayed, studied the Mormon teachings, repented, and worked at teaching others. Still, she never felt it was enough. She could never feel the conviction she thought she should. At age 26, married and with two children, she realized she could not accept the doctrine that made women subservient to men and that at times ran counter to historical facts. She came to think that what she had been told was not true. She says, "I'll never again surrender any part of my ability to think and study freely about a thing and draw my own conclusions. I love to learn, and I love not needing to first ask, 'What's the Church's position on this?'"[9]

loving God could let such bad things happen. They may become deists, those who believe in God but don't believe he actually takes a personal interest in each of the billions of individuals on Earth.

Others come to believe that the personal God of their faith is hypocritical or lacks morality. The God of the Bible's Old Testament, like the gods of the ancient Greeks, is often viewed as vengeful or murderous, qualities that are not accepted as moral in society. Some find that God's choosing of some people over others, thus relegating most of humanity to hell, is not fair. Others point out contradictions in the text of the Bible, which is said to be a divinely inspired document. Some people feel that ancient religious texts are not relevant to life today. Human rights, such as equal rights for women and racial minorities, are often not supported in religious texts.

Leaving a religion can be traumatic, especially for those who live in the United States, where religion plays such an important role. In other, more secular countries, such as Denmark and Norway, withdrawing from religious belief is a more common part of growing up.

Changing Times

Social scientists study all forms of culture, including professions, politics, and belief systems. Areas of interest for these scientists include how beliefs differ in different places. They also gather statistics on demographics, or how groups within a population are distributed. For example, the percentages of males and females in a specific profession, or the gender makeup of Congress, may not match the makeup of society as a whole. As the nonreligious community has grown over the last few decades, scientists have studied who is more likely to be a member of this community and how that is changing over time.

The majority of the nonreligious are educated people. Universities are traditionally places where ideas are freely shared and young people meet others with different worldviews. The educated are more likely to have read broadly, to have traveled, and to have an understanding of science. A 2006 survey showed that among American psychology and biology professors, 61 percent were atheist or agnostic.[10]

People who are nonreligious tend to be wealthier. This correlates with those who have more education; people who go to universities tend to make better salaries than those who do not. Countries with higher gross domestic products (GDPs), a common measure of a country's wealth, are more likely to be more secular, whereas the poorest countries tend to be more religious. The most secular countries include Canada, Israel, Japan, and those in Western Europe.

Universities are often home to a higher concentration of nonreligious people than might be found in the general public.

The nonreligious are predominantly white. Again, this correlates with geographic areas such as Europe, Australia, and Canada, which are more educated and wealthier than many countries in Africa or South America. Wealthy Asian countries also have high numbers of nonreligious people.

The nonreligious are mostly male. A 2014 survey from the Pew Research Center showed that 27 percent of men were nonreligious compared with 19 percent of women.[11] This may have historical

Millennials are less likely to be religious than members of other demographic groups.

reasons. Wealth and education tend to correlate with being nonreligious, and men were traditionally

provided with more education and controlled more wealth. Another reason may be that women

traditionally raised children, drawing on religion to teach morals and socialize with their communities.

Young and Progressive

Recent years show a marked increase in the number of people who identify themselves as unaffiliated with any religion. A Pew study showed that 22.8 percent of Americans identified as nonreligious in 2014 compared with 16.1 percent in 2007.[12] Approximately one-fifth of these nonreligious people were raised in a religion but later left it.[13] Today, the nonreligious are increasingly young. One in three millennials—people born between 1981 and 1996—in the United States is religiously unaffiliated.[14]

The nonreligious tend to have progressive politics. With the rise of the Christian right, a political movement that teamed conservative politics with evangelical Christianity, many young people began to view religion as aligned with conservative politics. Some young people and liberals view religions as judgmental and hypocritical. They often see religions as too involved with politics, money, and power.

As religion loses its influence, the question arises as to what will replace the aspects of religions that many people enjoy. Religion has had a central role in building communities, providing social opportunities, and engaging in charitable work. It has provided a sense of trust and tranquility. It has tied families together. One challenge for many secular individuals and families is to find ways to keep some of these benefits of religion in a secular community.

NONRELIGIOUS CULTURE

Historically, religion has given meaning to many people's lives. In some religions, the actions of individuals during their lives determine what happens to them after death. Moral actions please God, while immoral, or sinful, actions are punished by God. Guides to moral and immoral actions are written in texts inspired by God. Traditionally, under these religious structures, the purpose of life was to follow religious scripture to enter some form of afterlife. In other belief systems, actions in life affect a person's reincarnation, or rebirth, into other forms of life.

Although religion has historically given meaning to life, and still does for the faithful, this does not mean that the nonreligious do not have beliefs or that they feel their lives do not have meaning or value.

Rather than attending religious services, nonreligious people may set aside time for activities such as volunteering in their communities.

They have different ways of determining morality. They also have different ways of measuring value in their lives and understanding what happens after death.

Morality

There is often little difference in what are considered moral or immoral actions between the nonreligious and the religious on most issues. Both the religious and nonreligious generally consider lying, cheating, and hurting others as immoral. For the religious, these morals are laid out in laws such as the Ten Commandments or in parables from the Bible. For the nonreligious, these are acts with consequences to others in society.

The differences in what is moral or immoral between the religious and nonreligious tend to be acts that do not have consequences to others. Many personal acts such as drinking, dancing, or using offensive language are considered sins in some religions. Most nonreligious people do not consider private actions that do not affect others as immoral. They are more likely to believe that what people do in the privacy of their own homes is their own business.

Value

Many people seek belief systems in which they can feel there is some value to their lives. They want to feel that there is some importance to their time on Earth and that they can leave something behind after they die.

Raising children is one way nonreligious people may seek to add value to their lives.

For some nonreligious people, this value comes from making society a better place. They may work toward global equality or good stewardship of the planet. Others find value in their lives by raising a new generation that carries these values forward. Parents, grandparents, teachers, and others who work with children find value in their lives by ensuring a better future for society.

Others find immortality in material objects they leave behind. They may create art, architecture, or music that lasts long past their lifetimes. They may develop advances in science or medicine that make fundamental differences in people's lives. They may create new industries or develop new ideas that change society.

Death

The faithful of many religions are promised an afterlife. They may believe they will go to heaven and be reunited with loved ones who died before them. Although life is precious, death is not to be feared. Something better is ahead.

For most of the nonreligious, life is all there is. There is no afterlife. There is nothing to look forward to. For the nonreligious, death is the end. Despite this difference, researchers have noted that the religious are more likely than the nonreligious to request prolonged medical care when faced with a terminal illness. The nonreligious are less likely to prolong life artificially.

Community

People have an innate desire to belong. Traditionally, religious communities have filled this need to be part of a group of like-minded people. They have been the center of the community for the faithful, providing meeting places, holiday traditions, and rites of passage such as baptism, weddings, and funeral rites. As noted earlier, many people remain in religions because they enjoy the community.

Today, many nonreligious organizations are trying to fill the void created by leaving a religious community. Nonreligious groups are creating new customs. Some countries recognize secular weddings officiated by officials of nonreligious groups. Some humanist organizations write secular vows that members may use for wedding

EPICURUS AND DEATH

Epicurus (341–271 BCE) was an early philosopher who developed the theory that all things are made of tiny particles. He believed that people should enjoy their time on Earth, as that was all there was. Today, some of his words are popular at secular memorials. In one of his writings, he says,

Become accustomed to the belief that death is nothing to us. For all good and evil consist in sensation, but death is deprivation of sensation.

And therefore a right understanding that death is nothing to us makes the mortality of life enjoyable, not because it adds to it an infinite span of time, but because it takes away the craving for immortality.[1]

ceremonies. State laws in the United States vary, but most states require either a member of the clergy or a judge to officiate at a marriage.

Nonreligious people have also developed alternative secular versions of other rites, such as christenings, baptisms, or the Jewish bar mitzvah. An alternative to a traditional christening for babies is a naming ceremony. Naming ceremonies are generally attended by family and friends to introduce a new baby to the community.

Death rituals, such as the last rites in Catholicism, are central to many religions. Religious funerals center on the passage of an individual from this life to the next. Many nonreligious people instead choose to have memorials that are a celebration of the deceased person's life. Memorials often include the deceased person's favorite music or readings from favorite authors. They include personal stories from friends, colleagues, and family members, who ensure that the deceased person will live on in their memories.

CAMP QUEST

Camp Quest is a summer camp to which freethinking families can send their children. The camp encourages children to discuss big questions about topics such as the meaning of knowledge. It provides lectures about famous atheists such as Daniel Radcliffe, star of the Harry Potter movies. But mostly it provides nonreligious children with a safe space to discuss their beliefs. As one boy put it, he often felt uncomfortable with religious displays, such as praying before meals, when visiting friends. He bowed his head so he would not be rude but wondered if his friends would still like him if they knew he was an atheist.

The first Camp Quest began in 1996 for children ages 8 to 12. It has since expanded, with new camps for teens. By 2017, Camp Quest had grown to 13 affiliates across the United States and had partners in the United Kingdom, Switzerland, and Norway.[2]

Raising Nonreligious Children

For nonreligious parents, it is often difficult to find a balance between raising their children to think for themselves and indoctrinating them into their own secular beliefs. For secular parents, there will come a time when their children will ask about the God they have heard about from their friends. Striking a balance between denying the existence of other people's beliefs in God and encouraging children to think for themselves is difficult.

Raising a child to be a freethinker does not mean parents don't provide guidance. Secular parents may emphasize moral guidance in becoming an ethical, moral, freethinking, and self-respecting person without instilling a particular religious belief.

Secular parents also face social issues when interacting with religious friends or family. Many of their children's friends will go to Sunday school, pray before meals, or perform other religious acts in public spaces. Older generations in a family may be religious and consciously or unconsciously indoctrinate younger relatives into their beliefs. Secular parents must be prepared to explain why different people follow different traditions.

For secular parents, there are new educational materials that help guide the education of secular children. Traditionally, the study of philosophy, concerning such subjects as ethics, reasoning, and existence, has been reserved for students attending colleges and universities. Today, elementary and secondary school courses are available for parents

PERSPECTIVES

A MIXED COUPLE

When Kevin Zimmerman and his wife, Roseli, married, they both believed in God. But as time went on, Kevin began to think more about religion and eventually lost his faith. When he told his wife that he no longer believed in God, she was devastated. They had several children, and Roseli wanted the children to be raised in their religion. As Kevin says, "She wasn't comfortable with me being honest with the children about what I thought concerning religion, but I was just as uncomfortable pretending to be religious. Such an arrangement meant that Roseli could be authentic but that I could not."[3] Kevin could not agree. He felt that by keeping his own beliefs quiet he was contributing to the isolation felt by many atheists and the stigma that atheists face. Although the couple faced antagonism from some religious friends over Kevin's beliefs, they finally managed to gain a respect for each other's beliefs and could agree to disagree.

Camp Quest features traditional camp activities alongside science-based exercises in freethinking.

who want to encourage freethinking in their children rather than indoctrination.

In these classes, children are taught to exchange ideas and think about other people's ideas. The curriculum encourages self-expression and mutual respect. The Philosophy for Children cooperative supports freethinking families with curriculum developed and shared by its members worldwide.

The University of Washington now has a program, the Center for Philosophy for Children, that trains university students to take philosophy into K–12 schools. The program also holds workshops for parents and teachers.

The countries of Scandinavia are highly secular.

SECULAR SOCIETIES

Secular democracies are countries where there is a separation between church and state and where religiosity is relatively low. People in these countries identify as having a secular government rather than having one based upon Christianity, Islam, Judaism, or another religion. Many people are atheist or agnostic, and few believe in supernatural events. Religious participation is low, and there is relatively little observance of religious rituals and rites.

Secularists are not against the right of individuals to have a religious faith. But they do oppose religion or the religious being afforded privileges within a government. This may include public money used to fund religious schools or transportation to religious schools. It also may include religions being given tax-exempt status even though they are sometimes wealthy organizations that control large amounts of cash and real estate.

Countries that are secular tend to have high standards of living and strong governmental social programs that provide security for their citizens. These governments provide health care. They provide family services such as childcare and leave for new parents. Secular countries are statistically more peaceful and have lower murder rates than more religious countries do, including the United States.

The US Anomaly

The United States has seen rapid growth in the number of nonreligious people in recent years. Still, the country lags behind many other industrialized countries in the number of nonreligious citizens. In a 2014 Pew survey, 22.8 percent of respondents in the United States said they were atheist, agnostic, or "nothing in particular."[1] A Gallup poll in 2015 showed that in many countries in Europe, such as Germany, Sweden, and France, approximately half of people identified as nonreligious. Wealthy Asian countries also had a high percentage of atheists.

STATE-SPONSORED CHURCH, SECULAR NATION

The United Kingdom is one of the most secular countries in the world, with more than one-half of its people stating they are nonreligious.[2] But the country also has a state-sponsored church, the Church of England. It was established in 1534 by King Henry VIII in response to the pope's refusal to grant him an annulment of his marriage. The monarch is the head of the church. In the House of Lords, the upper chamber of Parliament, 26 seats are reserved for Church of England bishops. Today, some question the idea of having a state religion given the secular nature of the country.

On the other extreme, many countries in the Middle East, where the dominant faith is Islam, have governments heavily influenced by religion. In several of these countries, atheism is punishable by execution. In Turkey, often described as one of the more moderate countries in the region, atheists are sentenced to prison. African and South American countries have low levels of nonreligious people, with South Africa having 9 percent and Venezuela having one of the lowest numbers at 2 percent.[3]

The United States is an anomaly among other Western countries, maintaining a higher percentage of religious people. One of the most heated arguments in the United States is how much religions and other nonprofits should be responsible for social services. Religious institutions have traditionally provided social services for their own members. They also provide services for people outside their faith, often with a heavy dose of proselytizing. When funding for social services is provided by donations to a church, the religious

ISRAEL

Israel was founded as a Jewish state in 1948, partially in response to religious persecution against Jews around the world. A 2015 Pew survey found that 81 percent of Israelis considered themselves Jewish. The rest of the population is mostly Muslim. There is a great divide in Israel about the role of religion in the country. Approximately one-half of Jewish Israelis consider themselves secular. Twenty percent do not believe in God. Secular Jews prefer a separation of religion and state. Only approximately 20 percent, those who identify as Orthodox Jews, believe Israel should follow Jewish law rather than democratic principles.[4]

Towns in the United States are often home to churches representing a variety of religious denominations.

have a right to set the rules. But in recent decades, more and more funding for religious social services is coming from the government. The entanglement of church and state has increased in the United States in recent decades with the development of faith-based initiatives. Faith-based initiatives allow the government to give money to religious organizations that provide social services, such as feeding and housing the poor, as well as health or adoption services.

Office of Faith-Based and Community Initiatives

In 2001, President George W. Bush wrote an executive order establishing the Office of Faith-Based and Community Initiatives. In 2003, the government gave $1.17 billion to religious organizations.[5] Although the money was to be spent for social services, there were few rules about whether social services could be combined with religious practices.

In 2010, President Barack Obama put in new rules and oversight about religions using federal dollars to promote their faiths or hire people based on their faith. Still, money flowed to religious organizations, which sometimes spent federal funds on new buildings or infrastructure improvement. By 2015, the government was giving $210 billion each year to faith-based organizations.[6]

Many nonreligious people do not approve of their tax dollars funding religious organizations and may not feel comfortable depending on religious organizations for help. Therefore, when their federal taxes are given to church organizations, they are put at a disadvantage when they suddenly find themselves out of work, sick, or in need of immediate relief after a disaster. The social safety net

PERSPECTIVES

PRESIDENT BARACK OBAMA

US presidents have often struggled to balance their own faith-based values with the separation of church and state required by the US Constitution that they have sworn to uphold. President Barack Obama became a Protestant Christian as a young adult while working as a community organizer in Chicago, Illinois, believing that Jesus set an example for helping communities. But as president of the United States, he had to balance his own beliefs with those of people throughout the country. As Obama explained,

> Democracy demands that the religiously motivated translate their concerns into universal, rather than religion-specific, values. It requires that their proposals be subject to argument, and amenable to reason. I may be opposed to abortion for religious reasons, but if I seek to pass a law banning the practice, I cannot simply point to the teachings of my church or evoke God's will. I have to explain why abortion violates some principle that is accessible to people of all faiths, including those with no faith at all.... In a pluralistic democracy, we have no choice.[7]

is not there for them in the same way it is for the religious.

Eastern Religions

Eastern democracies also have growing numbers of nonreligious people. The largest religions in Asia, Hinduism and Buddhism, have hundreds of millions of followers each. The cultures and traditions surrounding them have become major parts of the societies they have touched. Still, the nonreligious people have a presence in these regions.

Hinduism, the world's oldest major religion, began approximately 3,500 years ago in India. Brahman, the main god of the Hindu religion, encompasses everything in the universe. In this religion, souls are said to move from one being to another upon death.

The path the soul takes is a result of good or bad decisions in a person's life.

Jainism, which began approximately 2,600 years ago in India, followed the Hindu belief in reincarnation but removed belief in any gods. Jains believe that all living things have a soul that should be treated with respect. Therefore, nonviolence toward all things is the main tenet of the faith. The approximately 4.5 million Jains believe the path to liberation of the soul depends entirely on the acts of the person.[8]

Buddhism began in India approximately 2,500 years ago. It is now widespread in Southeast Asia, Japan, China, and nearby areas. It is based on the teachings of Siddhartha Gautama, known as the Buddha. Buddhism does not recognize a god but centers on finding inner peace through meditation. Buddhists believe the mind is separate from the body. Upon a person's death, the body and conscious mind cease to exist, but an inner mind continues with no beginning and no end.

SOUTH KOREA

There is no dominant religious group in South Korea. In a Pew study in 2012, 29 percent of South Koreans considered themselves Christian, 23 percent considered themselves Buddhist, and 46 percent had no religion.[9] By 2015, according to a government statistics group, that number of nonreligious people had risen to 56 percent. The large increase primarily consists of young people who do not find religion important to their primary interests, which are often getting a good education and finding a job. Among those under 20 years old, 69 percent were nonreligious.[10]

Though Buddhism features no gods, its adherents often venerate the Buddha.

India has a secular democratic government. Fewer Indians are adhering to the ancient faiths than in the past. The 2013 Global Index of Religiosity and Atheism found 81 percent of Indian citizens consider themselves religious. This was a 6 percent drop from 2005.[11]

THE NEW ATHEISTS

In the early 2000s, a new group of atheists emerged in response to growing religious fundamentalism in the Middle East and the United States. These were not people who quietly pursued their beliefs. They were outspoken advocates of atheism and opponents of organized religion. They encouraged other freethinkers to be public about their atheist identities. Journalists nicknamed these thinkers "the New Atheists."[1] The New Atheists view religion as responsible for much of the intolerance in the world and believe that countering religious dogma with rational thought is the way to advance civilization and peaceful coexistence.

The Four Horsemen

A group of the most prominent New Atheists was nicknamed the "Four Horsemen." The name is a play on the Four Horsemen of the

Scientist Richard Dawkins is among today's most vocal supporters of atheism.

85

Apocalypse, found in the Christian Bible's Book of Revelation. The Four Horsemen of atheism were prolific authors and speakers. Their books became best sellers, and they became some of the most famous public atheists in the world. They were Christopher Hitchens, Daniel Dennett, Sam Harris, and Richard Dawkins.

ISLAMIC FUNDAMENTALISM

Islamic fundamentalism is a movement that began in the 1980s in several Muslim nations. Members of the movement resist Western influence on society and believe that the government should enforce strict interpretations of Islamic laws. Some members have resorted to terrorism as a tool against secular governments and the West. Many people equate all Muslims with those who follow Islamic fundamentalism. This is a false belief, as the vast majority of the world's Muslims do not agree with the ideas of Islamic fundamentalists.

Hitchens was a journalist, writer, and staunch opponent of religion. He was shocked in 1989 when Ayatollah Khomeini, a Muslim cleric from Iran, called for the murder of Hitchens's friend, author Salman Rushdie. Rushdie had written the book *The Satanic Verses*, which some Muslims believed was insulting to their religion's prophet, Muhammad. Hitchens began to write more about violence carried out in the name of fundamentalist Islam. The terrorist attacks of September 11, 2001, in which Muslim terrorists flew aircraft into buildings, further convinced him that the world had to address this growing threat.

Hitchens was known for his quick wit and wealth of literary knowledge.

Sam Harris incorporates research on the inner workings of the brain into his critiques of religion.

Hitchens's 2007 book, *God Is Not Great: How Religion Poisons Everything*, was a call to arms to counter religious dogma with reason. He explained the atheist position as follows: "Our belief is not a belief. Our principles are not a faith. We do not rely solely upon science and reason . . . but we distrust anything that contradicts science or outrages reason."[2] Hitchens died in 2011.

A Scientific Approach

The other three horsemen of the New Atheism are similarly outspoken, but they have science backgrounds. Daniel Dennett and Sam Harris both work in the field of neuroscience, the study of the nervous system. They have particular interests in how the brain thinks and reasons.

Dennett's 1995 book, *Darwin's Dangerous Idea: Evolution and the Meaning of Life*, proposes that the process of evolution can account for the human mind's ideas about morality. According to this theory, the mind, just like the body, has evolved to improve survival. In this case, it has done so by instilling morals. Dennett has also addressed self-awareness, artificial intelligence, and morality, asking questions about whether machines can gain these attributes.

Dennett has vehemently dismissed religious claims that fly in the face of scientific evidence. He has questioned whether clergy who make their livings promoting miracle cures and prayer healing should be treated the same as con artists who sell false cures for illness. At the same time, he appreciates some of the cultural aspects that religions have provided.

THE SCIENCE OF BRAIN IMAGING

Functional magnetic resonance imaging (fMRI) analyzes brain activity by measuring the blood-oxygen levels in different parts of the brain. The result of the imaging is a picture of the brain showing which areas are lit up, or being used more, during different brain activities. Scientists are using this new tool to investigate several questions dealing with religion and brain function. Early studies have researched the areas of the brain associated with religious activities such as meditation or religious thought. Particular types of mental activity, such as considering a moral problem, have been found to create specific patterns in the brain. Another group of researchers is interested in how artificial stimulants, such as certain drugs traditionally used in religious ceremonies, affect the processing of thought. Neuroscientists do not expect to answer the question of whether there is a God by studying the human brain. However, they do hope to understand how the brain works when thinking about questions typically considered religious.

Harris has also been a vocal advocate against religion. His 2004 book, *The End of Faith: Religion, Terror, and the Future of Reason*, is an analysis of faith versus reason. It warns against mixing politics and religion in a volatile world. In his scientific research, Harris has used new imaging techniques of the brain to study how the brain processes belief, disbelief, and uncertainty. Both Dennett's and Harris's research illustrate ongoing scientific work into understanding the physical processes in the brain that are behind the phenomenon of faith.

Richard Dawkins is an evolutionary biologist and perhaps the most well-known of the Four Horsemen. His most famous book, 2006's *The God Delusion*, argued that religious faith is a delusion, a false belief held even in the presence of contradictory evidence. The book reached number 4 on the *New York Times* best-seller list, selling millions of copies worldwide. Dawkins asserted that "atheists should be proud, not apologetic, because atheism is evidence of a healthy, independent mind."[3] Some have criticized Dawkins's approach. They contend that his attacks on religion sometimes amount to religious intolerance.

Dawkins was a key speaker at the first Reason Rally, held in 2012 on the National Mall in Washington, DC. Approximately 20,000 atheists gathered to showcase the growing number of nonreligious people in the United States.[4] The event featured scientists and many vocal anti-religious speakers. Many nonreligious people had a rare opportunity to meet other like-minded people and express their ideas openly.

REASON RALLY 2016

In 2016, a second Reason Rally was held in Washington, DC. The rally was much more inclusive than the initial rally in 2012, which had featured some strongly anti-religious speakers. Rather than bashing religion, organizers in 2016 hoped to bring a more diverse group together to support separation of church and state. The focus was also on issues such as gender rights, climate change, and other policies determined by humanism and reason rather than by a particular religious faith.

THE NEW HUMANISTS

The number of nonreligious people has continued to grow in recent years. Many seek a sense of community in the absence of organized churches. They may understand the reasoning behind the arguments against religious dogma, but they believe humans also have an emotional component to their lives. The New Humanists, those who center their endeavors on the human experience and community rather than focus on a rejection of religion, have tried to fulfill this need.

Some of these new communities are modeled on traditional church experiences. In 2013, events called Sunday Assemblies were organized by Sanderson Jones and Pippa Evans in London, England. They quickly spread to the United States. These meetings bring atheists together to reflect, sing songs, and help their communities. Religious participants are also welcome. The assemblies have

Sanderson Jones and Pippa Evans at a Sunday Assembly in 2015

expanded to include nonreligious weddings and other important ceremonies.

Paul Kurtz, founder of the Council for Secular Humanism, also recognizes the human need for a system of ethics and ritual. He encourages what he calls "secular spirituality," or finding an emotional dimension to life in the appreciation of music, art, nature, or meditation. Many people have found that even the study of science can bring on a sense of wonder and awe.

Some staunch atheists reject the notion of "secular spirituality," saying that it feels much too close to the religions they rejected. In a survey, Richard Cimino, professor at the University of Richmond in Virginia, and researcher Christopher Smith found that 23 percent of atheists surveyed refused to even consider a question about the subject of atheist spirituality. Of those who did answer, more than 40 percent agreed that they got a sense of wonder when contemplating art, music, or science. Almost 60 percent found such a sense when in nature.[1]

New Rituals

For those who enjoy the rituals or rites of passage found in religions, humanist groups have developed secular funerals, weddings, and naming ceremonies. Participants may write their own vows for weddings or material can be used from suggested materials written by the organizations. The nonreligious have developed their own holidays, too. Some celebrate the winter solstice rather than Christmas. The winter solstice is the day in the northern hemisphere with the shortest number of daylight hours of the year. To celebrate the lengthening daylight, the solstice is often celebrated with fires and lights. Hanging evergreens, holly, and mistletoe is also a solstice tradition.

A new holiday, Darwin Day, was created by Stanford University humanists in 1995 to

NONRELIGIOUS REPRESENTATION

In the US Congress, the nonreligious are severely underrepresented. Twenty-three percent of American adults are nonreligious, and the number is growing. But only 1 out of the 535 members of Congress, Arizona representative Kyrsten Sinema, is openly unaffiliated with a religion.[2] There may be several reasons for the low representation. Members of Congress tend to be older. A person must be at least 25 years old to be in the House of Representatives and 30 years old to be in the Senate. In 2017, the average age for senators was 61.[3] Many nonreligious people are members of younger generations. Another reason is that older citizens are more likely to vote. Seventy percent of those age 65 and older voted in 2012, compared with 38 percent for those under 24.[4] Finally, a high proportion of the American public remains suspicious of the nonreligious, and especially of atheists. In a 2014 Pew poll, more than one-half of Americans said that they would be less likely to vote for a presidential candidate who was an atheist.[5]

As part of Darwin Day celebrations in 2009, an actor portraying Darwin spoke to the media at the naturalist's grave.

celebrate science. Darwin Day has grown into an international holiday; its official website says it is meant "to inspire people throughout the globe to reflect and act on the principles of intellectual bravery, perpetual curiosity, scientific thinking, and hunger for truth as embodied in Charles Darwin."[6]

One of the largest secular gatherings is Burning Man, a celebration held in Black Rock Desert in Nevada each year. Participants celebrate art, community, free thought, philanthropy, and other expressions of what it means to be human. Larry Harvey founded the event in 1986. It has grown from a local event of 35 people on Baker Beach in San Francisco to a multimillion-dollar event in the Nevada desert welcoming people from across the world.[7] The event draws people from different religions, but 73 percent of the 2013 attendees were nonreligious.[8]

Still on Guard

Ellery Schempp, the young man who had fought for the separation of church and school in 1956, returned to his high school in Abington, Pennsylvania, in 2013 to accept an award. He was honored for his achievements in physics. Although he had thought back in the 1960s that the case was settled, by the 1990s Dr. Schempp had become concerned with efforts to return religion to schools. He realized there was still work to do. After he retired from his work in physics, he began speaking about his experience as a dissenter and urged others to remain on guard. He said, "Government and religion should not be intertwined, and when they are intertwined, individual Americans can feel oppressed."[9]

In 2012, he met with Jessica Ahlquist, a 16-year-old atheist who was fighting to have a religious banner removed from her school. More than 50 years after Schempp had taken a stand against religion in schools, Jessica was facing harassment from some in the religious community for standing up for her beliefs. On a talk radio show, a Rhode Island state representative called her an "evil little thing."[10] As she left school each day, she had to have the protection of guards because of threats she had received. Eventually, the school agreed to remove the banner. Ahlquist won a lawsuit, and the

As Schempp did decades earlier, Jessica Ahlquist won an important case related to the separation of church and state in public schools.

school decided not to appeal due to the expense of appealing the case.

Today, more people feel comfortable openly expressing doubts about religion. They still often face rejection and distrust from some in their communities, but they can also find more support from organized nonreligious groups. The religious will undoubtedly continue to find comfort and meaning for their lives in religion. But over time, as the nonreligious find greater acceptance and grow in numbers, they will become a more prominent part of culture both in America and around the world.

ESSENTIAL FACTS

TYPES OF NONRELIGIOUS PEOPLE

- Atheist: one who denies the existence of gods
- Agnostic: one who questions whether knowledge of God or gods can be known
- Freethinker: one who believes in using reason rather than faith to explore the world
- Humanist: one who believes in morals based on human welfare and dignity
- Secularist: one who believes that religion and the state should be separate

KEY EVENTS

- In 399 BCE, Socrates was put to death for heresy.
- During the Renaissance, scientists and philosophers questioned how the natural world worked, often resulting in contradictions with religious teachings.
- During the Enlightenment, scientists made significant advances in understanding how the world works, increasing tension with religious tradition.
- In the early 2000s, a new group of authors and thinkers, including four commonly known as the Four Horsemen of atheism, brought atheism further into the mainstream.

KEY PLAYERS

- Galileo (1564–1642) was an Italian scientist who challenged religious doctrine that held that Earth was the center of the solar system.
- Charles Darwin (1809–1882) developed the theory of evolution, which challenged religious beliefs.

- Ellery Schempp (1940–) is an American physicist who as a high school student fought for the separation of schools from religion.
- The so-called Four Horsemen of atheism are Christopher Hitchens, Daniel Dennett, Sam Harris, and Richard Dawkins.

NUMBER OF NONRELIGIOUS PEOPLE

As of 2012, 16.3 percent worldwide are unaffiliated with a religion.

- Asia/Pacific: 21.2 percent
- Europe: 18 percent
- North America: 17 percent
- Latin America: 7.7 percent
- Sub-Saharan Africa: 3.2 percent
- Middle East/North Africa: 0.6 percent

As of 2014, 23 percent of people in the United States are nonreligious.

QUOTE

"Democracy demands that the religiously motivated translate their concerns into universal, rather than religion-specific, values. It requires that their proposals be subject to argument, and amenable to reason. . . . In a pluralistic democracy, we have no choice."

—*President Barack Obama*

GLOSSARY

ANNULMENT
An official announcement that a marriage is invalid.

BOTANIST
A scientist who studies plants.

CIVIL LIBERTIES
Individual rights protected by law from unjust government interference.

DISSENTER
One who expresses an opinion different from others'.

DOGMA
A set of beliefs that is accepted by a group.

FUNDAMENTALISM
A form of a religion that follows a strict interpretation of the religion's texts and laws.

HERETIC
A person who has an opinion that is against established religious doctrine.

INDOCTRINATE
To teach someone to fully accept the ideas, opinions, and beliefs of a particular group and not to consider other ideas, opinions, or beliefs.

INTOLERANCE
An inability to accept views that are at odds with one's own.

NONDENOMINATIONAL
Accepted by any of the Christian denominations or sects.

PARANORMAL
Unable to be explained by science.

PERSECUTE
To treat people cruelly or unfairly, especially because of their religious or spiritual beliefs or their race.

PLAINTIFF
The one accusing a defendant in a court of law.

PROLIFIC
Producing many works.

PROSELYTIZING
Attempting to convert someone from one belief or religion to another.

SECULAR
Nonreligious.

TENET
One of the main principles of a religion or philosophy.

ADDITIONAL RESOURCES

SELECTED BIBLIOGRAPHY

Brewster, Melanie E., ed. *Atheists in America*. New York: Columbia UP, 2014. Print.

Bullivant, Stephen, and Michael Ruse, eds. *The Oxford Handbook of Atheism*. Oxford, UK: Oxford UP, 2013. Print.

Zuckerman, Phil, Luke W. Galen, and Frank L. Pasquale. *The Nonreligious: Understanding Secular People and Societies*. Oxford, UK: Oxford UP, 2016. Print.

FURTHER READINGS

Bodden, Valerie. *Understanding Christianity*. Minneapolis, MN: Abdo, 2019. Print.

Seidman, David. *What If I'm an Atheist?* New York: Simon Pulse, 2015. Print.

Tomley, Sarah, and Marcus Weeks. *Children's Book of Philosophy*. New York: DK, 2015. Print.

ONLINE RESOURCES

To learn more about the nonreligious, visit **abdobooklinks.com**. These links are routinely monitored and updated to provide the most current information available.

MORE INFORMATION

For more information on this subject, contact or visit the following organizations:

CAMP QUEST

PO Box 341
Staunton, VA 24402
540-324-9088
campquest.org

Camp Quest provides camping opportunities for the nonreligious.

FREEDOM FROM RELIGION FOUNDATION

PO Box 750
Madison, WI 53701
608-256-8900
ffrf.org

The Freedom from Religion Foundation works to protect the separation of government and religion.

SOURCE NOTES

Chapter 1. Establishment of Religion

1. Linda K. Wertheimer. "50 Years after *Abington v. Schempp*, a Dissenter Looks Back on School Prayer." *Atlantic*. Atlantic, 17 June 2013. Web. 16 Feb. 2018.

2. "First Amendment." *Legal Information Institute*. Cornell Law School, n.d. Web. 16 Feb. 2018.

3. "School District of Abington Township, Pennsylvania v. Schempp." *Legal Information Institute*. Cornell Law School, n.d. Web. 16 Feb. 2018.

4. "Religion in Public Schools: Engel v. Vitale." *Digital History*. University of Houston, 2016. Web. 16 Feb. 2018.

Chapter 2. Who Are the Nonreligious?

1. "Section 1. Population." *United States Census*. United States Census, 2012. Web. 16 Feb. 2018.

2. "Worldwide, Many See Belief in God as Essential to Morality." *Pew Research Center*. Pew, 13 Mar. 2014. Web. 16 Feb. 2018.

3. "The Sophists." *Internet Encyclopedia of Philosophy*. IEP, n.d. Web. 16 Feb. 2018.

4. "Italian Renaissance." *History Channel*. History, n.d. Web. 16 Feb. 2018.

5. Alan Cowell. "After 350 Years, Vatican Says Galileo Was Right: It Moves." *New York Times*. New York Times, 31 Oct. 1992. Web. 16 Feb. 2018.

Chapter 3. Breaking the Link between Church and State

1. Stephen D. Solomon. "The Kid Who Didn't Stand." *Tufts Magazine*. Tufts, 2007. Web. 16 Feb. 2018.

2. "Jefferson's Religious Beliefs." *Monticello*. Thomas Jefferson Foundation, n.d. Web. 16 Feb. 2018.

Chapter 4. Agnostics and Atheists

1. Jim Ketchum. "Edison's Spirituality Is More Similar to 'Scientific Deism.'" *Times Herald*. Times Herald, 10 Feb. 2017. Web. 16 Feb. 2018.

2. Joseph Kip Kosek, ed. *American Religion, American Politics*. New Haven, CT: Yale UP, 2017. Print. 104.

3. Thomas Henry Huxley. *Life and Letters of Thomas Henry Huxley*. New York: Cambridge UP, 2012. Print. 461.

4. "A Contribution to the Critique of Hegel's Philosophy of Right." *Marxists*. Marxists, n.d. Web. 16 Feb. 2018.

5. "Anti-Religious Campaigns." *Revelations from the Russian Archives*. Library of Congress, 31 Aug. 2016. Web. 16 Feb. 2018.

6. "Number of Atheists in Russia Halves in 3 Years—Poll." *RT*. RT, 25 July 2017. Web. 16 Feb. 2018.

7. Stephen Bullivant and Michael Ruse, eds. *The Oxford Handbook of Atheism*. New York: Oxford UP, 2013. Print. 562.

8. Jess Staufenberg. "The Six Countries in the World with the Most 'Convinced Atheists.'" *Independent*. Independent, 23 Mar. 2016. Web. 16 Feb. 2018.

9. Scott Bomboy. "The History of Legal Challenges to the Pledge of Allegiance." *Constitution Daily*. National Constitution Center, 14 June 2017. Web. 16 Feb. 2018.

10. "History of 'In God We Trust.'" *US Department of the Treasury*. US Government, n.d. Web. 16 Feb. 2018.

Chapter 5. The Nonreligious Revival

1. "Section 1. Population." *United States Census*. United States Census, 2012. Web. 16 Feb. 2018.

2. Gabe Bullard. "The World's Newest Major Religion: No Religion." *National Geographic*. National Geographic, 22 Apr. 2016. Web. 16 Feb. 2018.

3. Harriet Sherwood. "People of No Religion Outnumber Christians in England and Wales—Study." *Guardian*. Guardian, 23 May 2016. Web. 16 Feb. 2018.

4. Phil Zuckerman, Luke W. Galen, and Frank L. Pasquale, eds. *The Nonreligious: Understanding Secular People and Societies*. New York: Oxford UP, 2016. Print. 91.

5. Zuckerman, Galen, and Pasquale, eds, *The Nonreligious*, 91.

6. Zuckerman, Galen, and Pasquale, eds, *The Nonreligious*, 90.

7. Emily Brennan. "The Unbelievers." *New York Times*. New York Times, 25 Nov. 2011. Web. 16 Feb. 2018.

8. Melanie E. Brewster, ed. *Atheists in America*. New York: Columbia UP, 2014. Print. 146.

9. Brewster, ed, *Atheists in America*, 57.

10. Katharine Dunn. "Faculty Faith." *Harvard Magazine*. Harvard, 2007. Web. 16 Feb. 2018.

11. "America's Changing Religious Landscape." *Pew Research Center*. Pew, 12 May 2015. Web. 16 Feb. 2018.

SOURCE NOTES CONTINUED

12. Michael Lipka. "5 Key Findings about the Changing US Religious Landscape." *Pew Research Center*. Pew, 12 May 2015. Print. 16 Feb. 2018.

13. Lipka, "5 Key Findings about the Changing US Religious Landscape."

14. "America's Changing Religious Landscape."

Chapter 6. Nonreligious Culture

1. Stan van Hooft. *Life, Death, and Subjectivity: Moral Sources in Bioethics*. New York: Rodopi, 2004. Print. 175.

2. "Camp Quest: It's Beyond Belief." *Camp Quest*. Camp Quest, n.d. Web. 16 Feb. 2018.

3. Melanie E. Brewster, ed. *Atheists in America*. New York: Columbia UP, 2014. Print. 149.

Chapter 7. Secular Societies

1. "America's Changing Religious Landscape." *Pew Research Center*. Pew, 12 May 2015. Web. 16 Feb. 2018.

2. Harriet Sherwood. "People of No Religion Outnumber Christians in England and Wales—Study." *Guardian*. Guardian, 23 May 2016. Web. 16 Feb. 2018.

3. Phil Zuckerman, Luke W. Galen, and Frank L. Pasquale, eds. *The Nonreligious: Understanding Secular People and Societies*. New York: Oxford UP, 2016. Print. 563.

4. "Israel's Religiously Divided Society." *Pew Research Center*. Pew, 8 Mar. 2016. Web. 16 Feb. 2018.

5. "The Faith-Based Initiative Controversy." *The Jesus Factor*. PBS Frontline, n.d. Web. 16 Feb. 2018.

6. "Abuse in the Faith-Based and Community Initiative." *Secular Policy Institute*. Secular Policy Institute, 22 Apr. 2015. Web. 16 Feb. 2018.

7. Zuckerman, Galen, and Pasquale, eds, *The Nonreligious*, 175.

8. "Population by Religious Community." *Ministry of Home Affairs*. Government of India, 29 Dec. 2017. Web. 16 Feb. 2018.

9. Phillip Connor. "6 Facts about South Korea's Growing Christian Population." *Pew Research Center*. Pew, 12 Aug. 2014. Web. 16 Feb. 2018.

10. Steven Borowiec. "Why Young South Koreans Are Turning Away from Religion." *Al Jazeera*. Al Jazeera, 28 May 2017. Web. 16 Feb. 2018.

11. Kounteya Sinhal. "More Indians Have Stopped Believing in God: Survey." *Times of India*. Times of India, 27 May 2013. Web. 16 Feb. 2018.

Chapter 8. The New Atheists

1. Gary Wolf. "The Church of the Non-Believers." *Wired*. Wired, 1 Nov. 2006. Web. 16 Feb. 2018.

2. Christopher Hitchens. "God Is Not Great." *Slate*. Slate, 25 Apr. 2007. Web. 16 Feb. 2018.

3. Richard Dawkins. *The God Delusion*. Boston, MA: Houghton Mifflin, 2006. Print. 406.

4. Ruby Mellen. "Thousands of Atheists Gather in DC for 'Reason Rally.'" *CNN Politics*. CNN, 4 June 2016. Web. 16 Feb. 2018.

Chapter 9. The New Humanists

1. Richard Cimino and Christopher Smith. *Atheist Awakening*. New York: Oxford UP, 2014. Print. 126.

2. Danielle Kurtzleben. "Nonreligious Americans Remain Far Underrepresented in Congress." *NPR*. NPR, 3 Jan. 2017. Web. 16 Feb. 2018.

3. "The 115th Congress Is among the Oldest in History." *Quorum*. Quorum, 9 Nov. 2017. Web. 16 Feb. 2018.

4. Thom File. "Young-Adult Voting: An Analysis of Presidential Elections, 1964–2012." *US Census*. US Census, Apr. 2014. Web. 16 Feb. 2018.

5. Kurtzleben, "Nonreligious Americans Remain Far Underrepresented in Congress."

6. "What Is Darwin Day?" *International Darwin Day*. International Darwin Day Foundation, 2018. Web. 16 Feb. 2018.

7. "About Us." *Burning Man*. Burning Man, n.d. Web. 16 Feb. 2018.

8. Caveat Magister. "Burning Book Club." *Burning Man Journal*. Burning Man, 26 May 2014. Web. 16 Feb. 2018.

9. Linda K. Wertheimer. "50 Years after *Abington v. Schempp*, a Dissenter Looks Back on School Prayer." *Atlantic*. Atlantic, 17 June 2013. Web. 16 Feb. 2018.

10. Wertheimer, "50 Years after *Abington v. Schempp*, a Dissenter Looks Back on School Prayer."

INDEX

ABOUT THE AUTHOR

Cynthia Kennedy Henzel has a BS in social studies education and an MS in geography. She has worked as a teacher-educator in many countries. Currently, she works writing books and developing education materials for social studies, history, science, and students learning English. She has written more than 80 books for young people.